The House That Britten Built

How the Aldeburgh Festival brought music to Snape Maltings

by David Edwards

The House That Britten Built:

How the Aldeburgh Festival brought music to Snape Maltings

ISBN: 9780957676503

Author: David Edwards.

Published by Aldeburgh Music

Aldeburgh Music © 2013

www.aldeburgh.co.uk

Aldeburgh Music is a company limited by guarantee:

Registered in England and Wales number 980281

Aldeburgh Festival is a registered trademark ®

Snape Maltings Concert Hall, Snape, Saxmundham, Suffolk IP17 1SP

Editors: Inge Kjemtrup, Jane Bellingham

Design and cover: Silk Pearce

Printed by Five Castles Press, Ipswich

Printed on FSC certified paper.

Illustration acknowledgements at the back of the book.

Contents

Foreword

Taking visitors around Snape Maltings Concert Hall, I found that they were fascinated by its unique story – how East Anglia's largest industrial centre in Victorian times was re-invented in the 20th century into an internationally famous music venue, through the efforts of one of England's greatest composers, Benjamin Britten.

People always want to know what the building was like before it was converted into a concert hall, and they're curious about the infamous fire that followed, which threatened to destroy Britten's vision. They're also intrigued by the fact that artistic development at Snape Maltings has continued since Britten's death and that Aldeburgh Music's campus has turned Snape into Europe's leading centre for the development of young musicians.

This book attempts to tell that story.

But you cannot tell the story of the Concert Hall without telling the story of the Aldeburgh Festival itself, which was the very inspiration for the building's conversion. Alongside the fascinating saga of the Garretts and the insight into the daily life of a maltster at Snape, this book is also the story of Benjamin Britten and his partner Peter Pears, their original vision for a Festival in the small seaside town that they had made their home, and their inspired notion to turn a redundant malthouse into a world-class concert hall.

David Edwards
Suffolk, June 2013

CHAPTER 1
The Suffolk Coast

All where the eye delights, yet dreads to roam,
The breaking billows cast the flying foam
Upon the billows rising – all the deep
Is restless change; the waves so swell'd and steep,
Breaking and sinking, and the sunken swells,
Nor one, one moment, in its station dwells;
But nearer land you may the billows trace,
As if contending in their watery chase;
May watch the mightiest till the shoal they reach,
Then break and hurry to their utmost stretch;
Curl'd as they come, they strike with furious force,
And then re-flowing, take their grating course,
Raking the rounded flints, which ages past
Roll'd by their rage, and shall to ages last.

George Crabbe, *The Borough*, 1810

Billows breaking on the shingle at Aldeburgh beach

Fishermen have worked
off the Aldeburgh beach
from the earliest days.
This late-19th-century
fisherman is unloading
his catch of sprats

The eternal rolling of the North Sea has dominated the fortunes of the Suffolk town of Aldeburgh and the whole of England's eastern coast. Almost certainly a Roman settlement, and likely to have been a Saxon trading post from the eighth century, Aldeburgh (known as Aldborough, or 'Old Fort', until the 1880s) has long earned its living from the unpredictable sea. The sight today of fishermen hauling up their boats onto the shingle beach, landing, gutting and selling their fish, and repairing their nets is a daily replica of an ancient way of life, though much diminished in importance. Meanwhile, the rugged and ever-changing beauty of the seascape has inspired generations of artists, poets and musicians including Wilkie Collins, Thomas Hardy, George Crabbe, M.R. James, Benjamin Britten and more recently, Maggi Hambling.

Fish for sale on
Aldeburgh beach, 2006

Dunwich, to the north, became a thriving port in the 12th and 13th centuries. But as Dunwich disappeared beneath the sea and the changing coastline created a sheltered haven further south, the focus for ship building and trade shifted, and the town of Aldeburgh changed from a small fishing village to become the leading port on the East coast. Francis Drake's *Golden Hind* was built in Aldeburgh in around 1576, and for over a century, ship construction flourished in the area between the town and Thorpeness.

The Town Hall (rechristened Moot Hall in Victorian times) was built around 1550, and originally contained six small shops and a prison, as well as a meeting room for the town's burgesses. The Aldeburgh town council still meets there. The extension of the 15th-century Church of St Peter and St Paul over this same period is testimony to the wealth of the town at this time; built on the brow of the hill overlooking the sea, it was an important landmark for the 800 mariners recorded as working out of Aldeburgh at the time of Elizabeth I. Ship auctions were held in the nave of the church, and it is also said that touring theatrical companies performed here (although the story that Shakespeare himself may have played in Aldeburgh remains unproven).

However, the effect of the weather and the waves was gradually to silt up the access to the open sea, and the ship building industry declined. Disease, poverty and piracy combined to hit the community hard. A population of 1,300 in 1603 had reduced to approximately half that number by 1670. Coastal erosion meant the loss of properties close to the shore. In *Aldborough Described*, the Rev. James Ford wrote in 1815: 'From an accurate plan of the borough, which was taken in 1559, it appears that the church was then more than ten times its present distance from the shore.' The Moot Hall, once the centre of the market place, was now almost on the beach.

Located at almost the furthest eastern point in the country, Aldeburgh also faced the threat of human invasion from across the northern sea. In Elizabethan times, a map shows that cannon were situated on the beach, and there was a bulwark with five cannon at Fort Green, ready to face the Spanish threat of the Armada. In the summer of 1778, militia were stationed at Aldeburgh, ready to meet the Franco-Spanish threat of invasion in support of the American War of Independence. A few years later, the largest of a series of Martello Towers was built towards

Moot Hall, Aldeburgh, was built in 1550 as the Town Hall and still serves that function today. It once stood in the centre of the town

The 15th-century Church of St Peter and St Paul in Aldeburgh. Its position atop the hill made it a landmark for sailors returning home

the south of the town to resist Napoleonic forces, and concrete blocks and barbed wire defences were installed along the beach in the 1940s.

In the 19th century, the sea became Aldeburgh's friend again. The Marquess of Salisbury set up a home in Aldeburgh, which gave the town a new air of respectability. Soon wealthy holidaymakers, bored with the popular south coast resorts, were attracted by the health-giving properties of the Suffolk sea air. They brought new wealth to the town. Hotels, superior town houses and roads were built to meet the demand. Rev. Ford spoke of Aldeburgh's benefits: 'Vice has not yet erected her standard here, the society of Aldeburgh gay without profligacy, pleasurable without debauchery.' George Crabbe's son writes in his biography of his poet father that at the time that Crabbe was working as a surgeon in Aldeburgh during the 1770s, it was 'a poor and wretched place', but that this all changed with the 'elegance and gaiety' of the 'watering parties'. A railway branch line finally linked Aldeburgh with the rest of the expanding rail network in April 1860, firmly establishing the town as a holiday destination for the discerning 'excursionist' enjoying a visit to the sea. The construction of a pier opposite the Moot Hall, however, never reached completion, but for many years, bathing huts were a common sight on the beach alongside the fishing boats.

ABOVE: Cannon on the beach in this Elizabethan map show Aldeburgh ready for attack from the Spanish Armada

LEFT: By Victorian times, Aldeburgh had become a fashionable resort, with bathing machines and picnics on the beach

TOP: Heather and gorse on Snape Warren, where rabbits provided fur and food for the locals

LEFT: The River Alde meanders from Snape towards Aldeburgh, without ever actually arriving

BELOW: The route from Aldeburgh on the coast to Snape

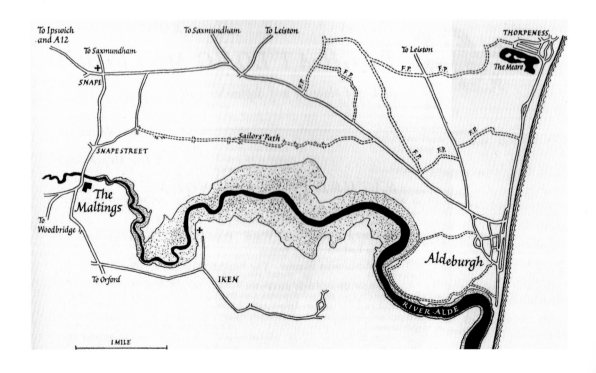

TOP: Villagers in Snape
have been baptized in
this font for around
500 years

LEFT: The church of
St John the Baptist,
Snape, dates back to
the early 15th century

Meanwhile, six miles inland, but connected by the River Alde, lies the village of Snape. The village sits at the highest navigable point on the river, which winds down past St Botolph's Church at Iken, never quite to reach the town of Aldeburgh but to take a sharp southward turn to become the River Ore and meet the sea south of Orford. Broad open skies over a meandering river, marshbanks edged with whispering reeds, heather and gorse on the common, the sound of birdsong, we can still sense the same timeless landscape that our ancestors enjoyed.

Snape's first entrance into recorded history is in the Domesday Book, where in 1086 it was noted that there was a church, standing in eight acres and valued at 16 pence, and that 49 men lived with their families in the village. Archaeology, however, takes us further back. Flint heads have been found on Snape Common, and a bronze axe head was ploughed up at Snape Watering in 1958. There is evidence that the Romans evaporated the waters of the River Alde to produce salt.

Excavations of tumuli along the Snape–Aldeburgh road a half-mile east of the church in 1862 discovered an Anglo-Saxon ship burial, dating from between 410 and 650. Bolts that would have fastened the ship's ribs clearly marked its outline, and inside was a skeleton with a gold ring on his finger, a sword and short blade of steel by his side, therefore presumed to be a chief. Locks of auburn hair remained, and there was a fragment of a comb. Another sixth-century grave excavated at Snape revealed a man turned into sand, lying on his back with a shield and a buckle, and, cradled in his arms, the remains of a six-stringed lyre: an early Snape musician. So we have a picture of an east-coast settlement, facing the mixed blessing of invasion by Romans, Angles, Saxons, Norsemen and Danes, who in their various ways all left their own legacy on this quiet part of England.

The original community settled on the higher ground, around the church, which was first built probably in the seventh century; however, in time, the village moved towards the river, where it was more convenient for work based around the tides, such as fishing and sea-trading.

Snape Church's East Window, designed by
Mary Lowndes in memory of Maurice Cowell,
shows the river at Snape Bridge

Snape Bridge today

In 1155, Benedictine monks founded a priory where Abbey Farm now stands, made possible by Norman landowner William Martell who gave his manors at Snape and Aldeburgh 'together with the benefit of wrecks from the sea between Thorpe and Orford Ness' for this purpose when he set off for the Third Crusade. The monks probably built the first wooden bridge over the Alde at Snape; by 1492 it was sufficiently in need of repair for the Bishop of Norwich to give permission for alms to be sought from travellers using the bridge to help with its maintenance. The first redbrick hump-back bridge was constructed in 1802, to facilitate transport to and from London. It was finally replaced in 1960; some of the original bricks were used for the bus shelter on the Aldeburgh Road, and Benjamin Britten is said to have reclaimed some for use in his garden at the Red House.

Cardinal Wolsey stripped the priory of its assets in the mid-1520s in order to establish his planned college in Ipswich, and little now remains. During Cromwell's protectorate, William Dowsing broke up 'popish' pictures and brassware in Snape Church, and in 1676, its thatched roof was destroyed.

From around 1800, Osborne and Fennell ran a corn and coal business at a small quay at Snape Bridge. This quay became a thriving port linking the east coast with London. Local produce was loaded on to barges at Snape, and the barges returned with coal and other goods for local distribution. A passenger sloop made a weekly voyage from the quay to London.

Snape was long associated with smuggling. Wines, spirits, silk, lace and tobacco were brought in from Holland and Belgium under cover of darkness. From the vantage point of the south-facing upstairs window at the Crown Inn, a watcher (it was apparently more profitable to be a watcher than an informer) signalled the all-clear to the smugglers once the customs officers were settled in the bar below.

The Post Office Directory of 1865 shows the extent of life within this 19th-century Suffolk village; butchers, bakers, farmers and grocers as well as a blacksmith, a wheelwright and a boot- and shoe-maker all had businesses in this small community.

Two local men from separate centuries will forever be linked to the joint history of Aldeburgh and Snape. Through their immense achievements, we can tell another story, which culminates in the Suffolk coast becoming an international musical centre, and Snape Maltings Concert Hall one of the world's most admired concert venues.

The six-mile Sailors' Path across the heathlands between Aldeburgh and Snape was renowned as a route for smugglers, carrying their booty inland from the port at Slaughden. It is a popular walking path today

CHAPTER 2

The Garretts and Snape Maltings

The Garrett family was pre-eminent in Aldeburgh throughout the second half of the 19th century. Described by East Anglian writer George Ewart Evans as a man of outstanding enterprise and energy, Newson Garrett (1812–1893) was the first Mayor of the Aldeburgh Corporation, and twice re-elected. For 40 years a bailiff, he was a JP, a commanding lieutenant of the local volunteer company, branch-chairman of the Royal National Lifeboat Institution, Lloyds agent and a freemason. He was instrumental, with his brother, Richard, in bringing the railway branch line into Aldeburgh, and left an architectural legacy to the town in Brudenell Terrace, Alde House and the development of Park Road, while his philanthropy is recognized in the creation of the Jubilee Hall. Yet his beginnings as a prosperous businessman lie in the village of Snape.

In nearby Leiston, the Garrett family had established a successful iron foundry, specializing in agricultural machinery. The elder son, Richard, was lined up to take over the family firm, so his younger brother Newson left for London to seek his fortune. At first he became a manager of a pawnbroker's shop in Whitechapel, but after the death of his father, the 29-year-old Newson Garrett returned to Suffolk to live at the Uplands in Aldeburgh, and with his inheritance purchased the corn and coal business at Snape Bridge from Robert Fennell in 1841.

This painting of Newson Garrett hangs in the foyer of the present-day Concert Hall

Newson Garrett, photographed in his robes in 1886, was the first Mayor of Aldeburgh

TOP: Garrett tie-rod at Snape Maltings. The building ties were manufactured by Newson Garrett's brother Richard's foundry at Leiston, while the bricks came from his own brickworks

LEFT: Garrett built this arch in 1859 to enable the wagon track to run into the Maltings site. Coke and coal were offloaded and stored just inside on the right. In the distance you can see the original Victorian dovecote

BELOW: The archway in 2012

Newson soon set about expanding his new business. In 1846 he built his first granaries on the quay, and, having acquired an interest in the Bow Brewery in London, seized the opportunity to begin malting at Snape in 1854, using the latest techniques such as ensuring correct temperatures and economy of labour. Within three years, he was shipping out to London 17,000 quarters of malt and 200,000 quarters of barley each year (a quarter being 64 gallons) in barges from Snape Bridge Quay.

The development of the business created a need for more buildings – silos to store the incoming barley, and malt-houses where the grain would be converted into malt. The first phase of the development of the site took place over 13 years from 1846, with the granaries at the front (the arch is dated 1859), providing employment for local bricklayers and carpenters. It is said that the front of the Maltings is curved because Newson himself marked out the boundary with his stick, and did not get it straight. As the business prospered, five malt-houses were erected, using bricks from the Garretts' own brickworks, and tie-rods cast at brother Richard's Leiston works. Newson built Snape Bridge House next to the Maltings for his family so they could live there during the winter malting season, with accommodation in the cellars for his servants (in the 1861 census, the Garretts had a cook, two housemaids, a footboy and a 61-year-old governess). As river traffic expanded, a carpenter's shop, a smithy and barge repair facilities were added. Across the main road from the Maltings, and in the village itself, Garrett bought over 20 houses, which were rented out to his workforce at favourable rates.

Originally, Newson relied on the river to transport his malt; he is reported as owning 12 of the 24 vessels registered at Aldeburgh. There could be three or four barges at the quay at any one time, awaiting the right combination of tide and wind to enable them to negotiate the narrow channel down to the sea, with others downriver at Iken awaiting a berth. However, even this could not keep up with the expansion of the business, so Newson persuaded the Great Eastern Railway to build a branch-line to the Maltings from Campsea Ashe. Eastern Counties Railway had been established in 1836, but it took an agreement with the Garrett brothers that they would guarantee regular goods traffic before the Snape line was built. It was opened on 1 June 1859.

Loading barges at Snape Quay, 1930s. The quay became a thriving port in the 19th century, linking Suffok to London and beyond

Steam train leaving the Maltings. The Snape line serviced the Maltings from 1859 until 1960

Victorian Snape – taken from the junction of Priory Rd and Church Rd, with the Golden Key in the centre

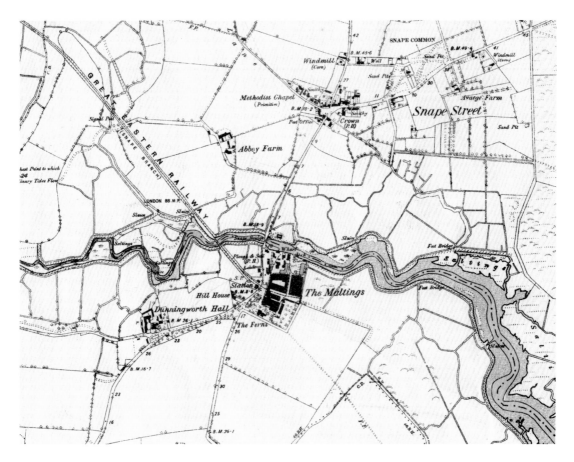

A map from 1881 showing the development of the Maltings around the
highest navigable part of the River Alde, and the diversion of the railway
to Snape

The line ran right into the site, although the engine itself stopped on the opposite side of the road, with the trucks being hauled into the Maltings by horses or ponies. A network of tracks throughout the site took the wagons to the wharf, to the stables and along the length of the front and rear of the granaries. There was a 13ft 6in diameter turntable in front of the main archway, and another in the middle of the site. The daily goods service travelled at only 15 m.p.h. but it greatly improved the ability of the firm to receive coal and coke for its furnaces and deliver malt to its customers as speedily as possible.

In 1882, the 27-year-old George, Newson Garrett's youngest son, became manager of the Maltings. With output growing, more buildings were constructed – the dates of 1884, 1885, 1890 and 1896 engraved into the buildings show the speed of the expansion, culminating in the last and biggest of the malt-houses, known as the 'New House', or Kiln No.5.

Newson Garrett died at Alde House in 1893 aged 81, and is buried in the churchyard of St Peter and St Paul Church in Aldeburgh. His epitaph in the church reads: 'God gave him largeness of heart.' His wealth at his death amounted to £50,605 net, worth over £5 million today. He left a remarkable legacy. Of his ten surviving children, Elizabeth became the first woman in Britain to qualify as a doctor and was the country's first woman mayor (in 1908, in Aldeburgh); Agnes was London's first woman interior designer; while Millicent married Henry Fawcett MP, played a leading part in the suffragist movement and was made a Dame in 1929.

Newson Garrett memorial in Aldeburgh Church.
He made a great contribution to the life of both
Aldeburgh and Snape

The Garretts also played a significant role in the life of Snape. They donated the village hall and rebuilt the school – to which George Garrett's wife Louisa introduced toothbrushes. A plaque outside the school surely reflects the Garrett philosophy; it reads: 'Even a child is known by his doings whether his work be pure and whether it be right'. But with benevolence remained status: it is said that as they drove through the village in their pony and trap, the Garretts expected the villagers to bow as they passed.

In 1910, George Garrett handed over the management of the Maltings to his nephew Maurice Cowell, but when war broke out, Maurice enlisted, and was killed in 1916. One hundred and seventeen men from Snape, many of whom would have worked at the Maltings, are listed in the church as having gone to serve 'for king and country'; a plaque commemorating Maurice Cowell together with 25 other Snape men who did not return, is in Snape Church, along with a stained-glass window commissioned in his memory. George came out of retirement to face the problems brought about by the war; the Ministry of Food ordered Snape to stop malting, as the barley was to be taken by the government for milling and the buildings used to store wheat instead. When a licence to make malt again was eventually issued in November 1917, it was late in the season, and the quality of the barley was poor. As a result, only two-sevenths of its pre-war output was achieved that year, badly affecting the viability of the business.

In 1918, George decided to merge the business with S. Swonnell and Son, a company based in Oulton Broad. George became chairman and remained so until his death in 1929, at which time there were still some 140 local men employed directly at the Maltings.

Strikes in the autumn of 1919 and again in 1924 began a decline in the fortunes of the railway, with a gradual shift to road transport. Barge traffic ceased during the early years of World War II and by the 1950s, the rail line was being used only for the delivery of coal to the Maltings once a week. The branch finally closed on 7 March 1960 – three years before the infamous Beeching Report – and the tracks were removed the following year.

During World War II Snape was scheduled as a Defence Area, and its children evacuated further inland. Several bombs fell on the village – the enemy thought the Maltings was a munitions factory – but no one was injured. Many of the men working at the Maltings again went to war, and local women were drafted in to take over their work.

The staff of Snape
Maltings pose for a
photograph outside the
front on 21 June 1900

The last building to be constructed on the site was the 'New Barley Store' in 1952, situated behind the Plough and Sail. In 1959, celebrating 100 years of malting at Snape, a party was held in the village hall and each man given an engraved tankard. However, modern techniques in the industry made the traditional Snape Maltings operation increasingly non-viable, and only six years later, S. Swonnell & Son went into voluntary liquidation. Commander Wood, chairman and senior managing director, told the *East Anglian Daily Times* (6 May 1965): 'It is quite impossible for us to continue to go it alone, particularly as Snape Maltings are so old-fashioned with their scattered buildings that they do not lend themselves to mechanization, except at enormous expense, which we cannot provide'. The next month it was closed, and some 50 men made redundant.

Soon, however, a new sign appeared above the archway at Snape Maltings: 'Gooderham & Hayward Ltd. Animal Feed Specialists and Grain Merchants'. The Gooderham family had long-standing links with Snape Maltings; during the 1880s George Gooderham had run a small mill supplying a circle of fellow farmers. Some of the barley he grew at that time was sold to Newson Garrett at Snape. The business passed down through the family, and became Gooderham & Hayward, the animal food compounders, working from a mill beside the railway line at Marlesford. In 1965 George Gooderham (Investments) Ltd bought the Maltings complex, together with the Plough and Sail, 27 other dwellings in the village and 32 acres of land. It took on many of the men who had been made redundant by Swonnells.

New machinery was installed, and milling commenced. A channel was dug in the river, and barge traffic was re-introduced, bringing bulk barley from Lowestoft. But the plans of the new owners did not include using the former kiln behind the main block, known as the New House, and its 11,000-ton storage capacity was advertised in the local press. Only time would tell who would come forward to take on what was by now a semi-derelict building.

CHAPTER 3

Life at the Maltings

Malt is produced by the germination and fermentation of barley. It is a key ingredient in the manufacture of beer – it provides the sugar on which the yeast feeds during the brewing process – but it also has other valuable uses.

After the annual harvest, barley was delivered to Snape Maltings from both local farms and abroad, by barge, road and, after 1859, by rail. Over the course of the malting season, which ran from October to May, the grain was put through a number of processes. First it was dressed, or cleaned, then soaked in water, or steeped, for up to four days to swell the grain, the water being changed at regular intervals. The wet grain was then spread out to germinate on concrete bays, kept at a constant temperature of around 70°C and regularly turned with wide shovels to achieve aeration. During this process, the hard grain changed to soft, sweet malt. After about eight days, when the grain had started to shoot, it was spread out to dry in the kilns, over perforated floors heated from below by coal furnaces. Heat was gradually increased over around five days, to halt any further germination, with the maltsters again regularly turning the grain using wooden shovels. On the last day of the process, the bluffs in the roof were opened to release the steam, and the sweet smell of malt wafted over the village. The malt was then cleaned of its rootlets, and stored until ready for despatch.

Following the merger with S. Swonnell & Son in 1918, an agreement was drawn up with the maltsters: their hours were to be 5am to 5pm (4pm on Saturdays), except for the dark nights from December to February, when they could leave at 4pm – 'unless needed'. Weekly pay was 38/- for boys, 57/- for 'Greenhands', 60/- for Floormen, and 65/- for Kilnmen. There was extra pay for porterage to and from the barges, an additional 5/- per kiln for cleaning and an extra 2/- per month if no time was lost. Kilnworkers were supplied with two pairs of canvas slippers.

At the end of October 1925, the workers threatened to strike over pay. Twenty-four maltsters gave 14 days' notice, demanding a rise of 5/- a week, a 20/- bonus paid for every 100 quarters of malt shipped out (twice the existing rate), and – almost as an afterthought – two pints of free beer a day. The management stood firm, and eventually the strike was called off on 4 November, with the workers settling for shorter hours.

Bob Ling – later employed at Snape as concert hall manager – began work at the Maltings in late 1938 at the age of 15. He was the third generation of his family to work there and began as one of the day-gang, getting 36/- a week, turning the barley to help it to germinate. His descriptions of life as a maltster were recorded by Eric Crozier, co-founder of the Aldeburgh Festival:

'When I started work at 15, I had to learn how to carry a coomb of malt – 12 stone: that was my O-levels. For my A-levels, I had to carry a coomb of barley – 16 stone. You had to learn how to carry them up a plank into a truck and how to spring with the plank: you had to get it nicely balanced on your shoulders and that helped you to walk.

'For getting the barley from the turning-bay to the floor of the kilns, we used barrows without wheels – long wooden barrows with handles at both ends. When you wanted to move your "piece" further on, you used a can of water to wet the concrete so your barrow would slide. Then you filled the barrow, got down and lifted that tremendous weight with your shoulder, then pushed – and then you tipped it out. The same barrows were used for emptying the kilns. The malt came up the elevators ... and there would be four men barrowing the malt onto the elevator down below, and three men up above in the kiln emptying the malt down the spouts.'

Spider Alexander, kiln worker. These photographs of the maltsters, holding the tools of their trade, were all taken c.1890 when Snape Maltings was at the height of its output

Andrews was a carpenter on site; the carpenters made all the tools for the Maltings, and lived in a company house, Wink's House

Andrews' son, Alfred, was an apprentice carpenter, working with his father

Tom Savage was a foreman maltster; he is holding the 'cot' of a 'turner', a flat-edged wooden tool for turning the barley

Harry Chaston was a roaster, but also a bricklayer – the maltsters had to turn themselves to many tasks, depending on the cycle of the year. His apron is made of sacking

Harry Puttock, gardener

Bob Ling, who had worked at Snape as a maltster, became the Concert Hall caretaker with his wife Doris, and in their retirement continued to take groups round the Hall and entertain them with their stories of life at the Maltings

At Snape, two types of malt were produced: pale malt and crystal malt. The pale malt was dried in the kilns in the New House, but the crystal malt – used for dark beers, but also other products such as Ovaltine – was cylinder-dried over coke fires. Bob Ling described life in the engine room 'with temperatures up to the skies':

'You had to stoke your furnaces and slice them. They were on rails: you pushed them along with your feet, so you could take the slides off the cylinders and tip the malt out, then re-load them – then you put the slides back and moved the furnaces under again. It was quite a skilful job testing the malt. You had a long spoon and you pushed it into the cylinder and got some malt on the palm of your hand and you could more or less tell by the colour whether it was cooked. There were five sacks in each cylinder and it took roughly an hour and a half to cook: two of us were in charge of the four cylinders of crystal malt. The other kind, the pale malt, took four days in the kiln. It looked like a tropical forest when the wet barley was giving off all its dampness – it was terrible! With four of you in a row turning the grain you couldn't see each other. Everything was soaking wet and you could see steam coming out of the "bluffers" or chimneys.'

Although the trains came to Snape in 1851, they were not routed through the site: wagons drawn by horses criss-crossed the Maltings. Here, Herbert Smith leads Mike and Prince pulling a wagon, either of coal for the furnace, or malt for onward transport

Eventually, horses gave way to motorized transport; here a tractor waits for the green flag before crossing the road to the station. Kitty Crane is waving the flag, Herbert Smith is driving and Maltings manager Cyril Smyth is looking on

Bob recalled that they wore aprons made of sacks, and tied straps or strings around their legs below the knee, in order to stop the mice running up the inside of their trousers. In fact, the maltsters could earn extra money from the rat population; presenting a rat's tail earned them an additional 3d.

Ray Poacher from Blaxhall started aged 16 as a pony boy, like his father and grandfather before him. He cycled in each morning and spent the day loading coke from the train trucks by hand into the pony and cart to move it to the storage bays. When Bob Ling was called up to join the navy, Ray took over his job in the engine room, qualifying for 'men's money' of £6 per week. He remembers the malt being red hot when it was being cooked, and says that compared to work on the farms – the main alternative employment – this was good money: but you earned it because of the heat in which you had to work. On firing-off day, the temperature reached 220°C. Bonuses were still being given for unloading the trucks, and the men also received an oval brass disc to exchange for beer at the Plough and Sail. Despite being so well looked-after, all the maltsters took on additional jobs to supplement their income. Some would have a meal, then go to work for local farmers in the fields. (Reputedly,

Local women joined the workforce in the war years. Back row, l to r: Ellen Ling, Leah Taylor, Sylvia Bloomfield; front row, l to r: Gwenny Crane, Kitty Crane, Peggy Airey

Collecting heather: heather was gathered on Snape Warren to use in the maltings furnaces

the first sugar beet to be grown in England was planted in the field next to the Crown Inn in Snape in 1911 by the landlord, Ted Pryke.)

Barges continued to visit Snape until the outbreak of war in 1939, when road transport became the main means of barley arriving at the maltings; Robert Simper tells the story of delivering such a load:

'At Snape there was the business of going into the office and having the sample on the lorry checked with the sample that had been bought. This over, I set off to find the foreman. I remember going into the dark malt floors and hearing the scraping of barn shovels on the cement floors above me. I climbed up numerous ladders, the hum of conversation growing nearer. There were perhaps half a dozen men, all wearing the maltsters' canvas rope soled boots and faded blue overalls, turning barley with side shovels.'

The furnaces were fired up using heather from Snape Common. Coal and coke for keeping the furnaces going were delivered by the railway, to the station in front of the Maltings. The engines however were not allowed to cross the road, so up to the mid-1950s Suffolk Punch horses were used to shunt the trucks, and there was always a pony to bring coke up to the engine room. A horse would manoeuvre the massive trucks carrying the malt sacks along the track that ran from the malt store to the quay. On reaching the quay, the horse was trained to swivel it round so that it could be offloaded into the barge, using a specially-made collar, which when pressed against the side of the truck would release the trip gear, sending the sacks down into the hold. Later, a tractor replaced horsepower, but the loading and unloading of the trucks remained back-breaking work.

Working as a maltster could also be dangerous. In 1922, James Hudson, a labourer, was wheeling a barrow of coal along the front of the Maltings, when a coomb of barley fell from its chain as it was being hauled into one of the projecting lucams, and crushed him. John Smith, a shunter, died after he slipped and fell under the wheels of a truck of cinders in 1930. Fires were also a hazard and Snape Maltings' own fire brigade was created in 1918 to deal with minor fires on site, remaining in service until 1964.

When Swonnells announced the redundancies in 1965, it came as a surprise to the workforce; they were not at all aware of the decline in the industry. The local paper reported: 'the news is a severe blow to the parish of Snape, which has relied for so many years on the fortunes of the maltings'.

CHAPTER 4
Benjamin Britten and the Aldeburgh Festival

'My music now has its roots, in where I live and work.'

  -Britten, on receiving the first Aspen Award, 1964

In April 1938, a young man whose future was to become forever linked to that of Aldeburgh, Snape and the Maltings, came to live in the village: 'I think I have found a good spot to live in – it is an old mill house in a quaint old village called Snape. It has a grand view...'

The grand view would have included, of course, the working Maltings.

Hudson's Mill, on the crown of the hill at the centre of the village, had closed in 1933 having been a working mill for well over a century. It was bought by Benjamin Britten, together with the adjacent granary and miller's cottage, with money inherited from his late mother.

At 24, Britten was already enjoying some success as a composer. Born in Lowestoft, 30 miles up the Suffolk coast, on 22 November 1913 – the day of St Cecilia, the patron saint of music – Britten had shown promise as both a performer and a composer from a very early age; he recalled having already written over 100 compositions by the time he was 12. The house in which he grew up faced the biting winds of the North Sea, and one of his childhood compositions was a tone poem inspired by a shipwreck. He was greatly inspired by the composer Frank Bridge, having been 'knocked sideways' by hearing Bridge's orchestral suite *The Sea* in Norwich in 1924 at the age of 11, and some three years later, he was taken on by Bridge as a composition pupil. At Gresham's School in Norfolk he learnt the viola and continued to compose, and won a scholarship to the Royal School of Music, where he studied from 1930 to 1933, winning numerous prizes. His official Op.1, Sinfonietta for chamber orchestra, was first performed in 1932, and the BBC broadcast his Op.2, the oboe quartet *Phantasy* that same year.

From 1935 to 1939, Britten worked as house composer for the GPO Film Unit, writing scores for nearly 20 documentary films, including *Night Mail*, for which his friend the poet W.H. Auden had written the words.

Not long after the death of his mother in the spring of 1937 Britten met the tenor Peter Pears, at that time a member of the BBC Singers. They were mutual friends of Peter Burra, and the two were thrown together following Burra's untimely death as they sorted through his affairs together. By September Britten had written his first song-setting for Pears, and they moved in together into a flat behind the BBC in 1938.

Meanwhile, 'Snape is just heaven', wrote Britten. The conversion of the Mill was designed for him by his sister's future father-in-law, Arthur Welford, who lived at Peasenhall Hall. The ground floor was turned into a circular studio, dominated by a grand piano. Above the studio was a bedroom, and to take advantage of the

Benjamin Britten at the beach with his mother. The sea remained a strong influence on Britten throughout his life

Britten at the piano in his childhood home, 1921

ABOVE: Hudson's Mill as it was in Victorian times. The Mill was built in 1797–8 and remained a working mill – one of three in Snape – until 1925

CENTRE: Britten at the converted Old Mill. The panoramic windows looked out towards Snape Maltings

BELOW: The Old Mill today

position of the mill on the brow of the hill, the roof was raised and large windows created to look out towards the river and Snape Maltings. As Britten worked on his composing, he would have smelt the sweet malt on the breeze, and seen the daily comings and goings at the Maltings.

Pears's reports from his singing tours to America inspired Britten to want to cross the Atlantic himself, and he became increasingly interested in American music. Aaron Copland came to stay in Snape, and passers-by could have heard the visitor playing through his school opera, *The Second Hurricane*, on Britten's grand piano. So when Britten received an offer from Paramount Studios in Hollywood to write the score for a projected film of *The Knights of the Round Table*, he leapt at the chance to further his career in the New World. With both Pears and Britten declared pacifists, the apparent imminence of war was an added incentive to be away from Europe. But in a letter he wrote while still on the voyage over, he said 'the more I think of Snape ... the more I feel a fool to have left it all', and it was the lure of his native Suffolk that brought Britten back some three years later.

While in California, Peter Pears had come across a copy of Suffolk poet George Crabbe's *The Borough*, with its story of Peter Grimes. Reading an article by E.M. Forster about it in *The Listener* magazine, the two men realized not only that it would make a good subject for an opera — Britten's first — but that its setting, Suffolk, so evocatively described by Crabbe, was where Britten belonged. And so they returned to England, and it was at the old mill in Snape where Britten went on to compose *Peter Grimes* (1945), *The Young Person's Guide to the Orchestra* (1946), *The Rape of Lucretia* (1946), and *Albert Herring* (1947).

In her biography of Britten, written in 1966, Imogen Holst described the lure of the Suffolk coast: 'On a stormy day, even in summer, the grey sea batters itself against the shelf, dragging the shingle down with a scrunching, grating, slithering sound. To anyone who lives on the Suffolk coast, this sounds means home.' Laurens van der Post, writing a decade later, also noted the particular lure of Suffolk to the artist: 'There is a kind of communion between man and his surroundings, a kind of partnership between the human being and nature, an exposition of harmony and rhythm of natural forces that I find nowhere else in the British Isles.' It was that feeling of belonging that brought Britten home to Suffolk, and that communion with the Suffolk coast that was to influence so much of his future work.

Britten and Pears at Crag House, Aldeburgh, 1954

FAR LEFT: Britten and Eric Crozier on the beach at Aldeburgh in the same year that they, together with Peter Pears, founded the first Aldeburgh Festival

LEFT: E.M. Forster giving a lecture in the Aldeburgh Baptist Church during the first Festival. Britten – whose return from America was prompted by reading Forster's article on George Crabbe – is to his right

With increasing royalties from his successful compositions, Britten bought Crag House in Aldeburgh in 1947 (although he continued to own the Mill until 1955). In this house, which overlooked the beach, Britten could compose while just outside the window, gulls would swoop over the fishermen as they unloaded their catches on the shingle beach.

However, the work of Britten and Peter Pears with the English Opera Group (which they had founded with the producer/librettist Eric Crozier and designer John Piper in 1947) frequently took them away from home, and it was while they were on tour in Holland and Switzerland with *Albert Herring* and *The Rape of Lucretia* in August of that year, that Peter Pears famously said 'Why not make our own Festival? A modest Festival with a few concerts given by friends? Why not have an Aldeburgh Festival?'

Why not indeed – particularly when just a few doors down from Crag House was the Jubilee Hall as a potential venue. And so it was that, after a great deal of debate and discussion with local friends and acquaintances, the Aldeburgh Festival of Music and the Arts was born, under the joint artistic direction of Benjamin Britten, Peter Pears and Eric Crozier. On 5 June 1948, the first Festival opened at Aldeburgh Church with Britten's *Saint Nicolas*, immediately starting a tradition of presenting new work by Britten, and incorporating both professionals and members of the community. The festival had to be mounted on a shoestring – apparently, Britten himself cut off the legs of one of his own wardrobes to make it fit into the church as one of the rostra. The Festival lasted for nine days, and included art exhibitions, talks – including one by E.M. Forster on George Crabbe – recitals, concerts and poetry readings.

Given that Britten, Pears and Crozier's friends were some of the world's leading musicians, it is perhaps not surprising that the Festival was an instant success, although this could not necessarily have been predicted. The late 1940s were still a dark period, following the austerity of wartime; milk, bread, potatoes, tea, sugar, eggs, cheese and meat were still rationed, as was petrol. Surrounding farmland was covered in weeds, the shingle beach littered with barbed-wire war defences, and there was limited accommodation for visitors. 1947/48 had been a very hard winter, and neither could the days of early June be guaranteed to be always sunny, with a fierce wind often blowing in to batter concert-goers taking their interval from the Jubilee Hall on the beach. It was not practice at that time to use churches for public performances, and yet the availability of Aldeburgh Church as a venue for concerts was critical to the Festival's schedule. However, the first festival was indeed a success, and the beauty of the setting, the coherence of the programme, the lure of outstanding artists and the chance to see and hear the developing work of Britten himself – emerging after the success of *Peter Grimes* as Britain's leading composer – immediately established Aldeburgh as a world-class festival, albeit with its roots firmly based in the local community of Suffolk.

The English Opera Group provided the opera performances for the early Festivals, starting with *Albert Herring*, with Peter Pears in the title role. The singers and instrumentalists would become the core artists for the Festival, joined by distinguished soloists, ensembles and local choirs. In addition to the music, there would be lectures, plays and poetry readings, as well as art exhibitions. Britten himself would be an indefatigable contributor, as conductor, chamber musician and accompanist, particularly for Peter Pears, who in the early years would sing almost daily during the Festival.

From the beginning, the Festivals were characterized by an eclectic range of music, from the classical period – Schubert, Haydn, Mozart, Purcell – to contemporary work, with young composers in particular being commissioned: the very first Festival featured a work by the 21-year-old Arthur Oldham, Britten's only private pupil (who went on to found the Edinburgh Festival Chorus). Challenging *musique concrète* was introduced to British audiences at the 1954 festival. The appointment of Imogen Holst as joint artistic director in 1956 introduced early choral music into the programme. The Festival brought to Suffolk such well-known artists as Janet Baker, Julian Bream, Osian Ellis, Kathleen Ferrier, Dietrich Fischer-Dieskau, Sviatoslav Richter, John Shirley-Quirk and Robert Tear. Britten's work featured in every Festival. His children's opera *The Little Sweep* was written especially for the Festival in 1950, as was *Noye's Fludde* in 1958. Soon, Britten would be writing at least one new piece for the Festival each year. His opera *A Midsummer Night's Dream* was premiered at the newly enlarged and refurbished Jubilee Hall in 1960. Britten met the Russian cellist Mstislav Rostropovich that year, and there began a long relationship with the Aldeburgh Festival. In 1964, Rostropovich played the first performance of Britten's Cello Symphony in Blythburgh Church.

As the Festival grew, so did its ambition. From its very first year, the directors had the vision of Aldeburgh as a centre for the arts, with its own theatre. Although part of the Festival's unique charm lay in its informal and often somewhat makeshift settings, the lack of a hall that could accommodate a large orchestra, and indeed a large paying audience, was increasingly seen as a drawback. As early as 1954, plans were drawn up for a brand new concert hall to be built in Aldeburgh on a site to the south of the parish church. But a decade later, the costs of erecting such a building were still proving prohibitive, and the project seemed to have no chance of moving forward. Was the future of the Aldeburgh Festival to be confined forever by its existing venues?

Britten and the Russian cellist Mstislav Rostropovich rehearsing in Moscow. The partnership between the two resulted in the Cello Symphony and the Sonata for Cello and Piano. Rostropovich later became an artistic director of the Aldeburgh Festival.

CHAPTER 5

From Maltings to Concert Hall

In 1965, Festival manager Stephen Reiss was looking for somewhere to store the English Opera Group's growing stock of scenery, when he spotted George Gooderham's advertisement for available warehousing at Snape Maltings.

The Aldeburgh Festival had long had the ambition for a permanent concert hall, and Britten was increasingly frustrated that without a bigger venue, the Festival was 'getting too emaciated without the capability of doing works with larger forces'. The empty late Victorian 'New House' building caught Britten's imagination: he was thoroughly familiar with the site from his days living in Snape. Although some of his colleagues felt it was a risky venture, Britten was determined that this could be the answer to the Festival's needs. Reiss contacted civil engineer Ove Arup, whose company had been responsible for the restoration of Coventry Cathedral – the setting for Britten's *War Requiem* three years before. Derek Sugden of Arup Associates was put in charge. As a Festival-goer since 1957, he knew the buildings, having regularly driven past them on his way to Aldeburgh.

George Gooderham welcomed the addition of the Aldeburgh Festival to the Maltings. He recalls walking around the site with Britten. At first, he remembers, the ideas were modest, but when they realized the opportunity, particularly given the ambience of the setting, the plans grew.

There were no models to follow; the idea of converting a former industrial building for this kind of purpose was quite new. The aim was 'to create a concert hall with certain facilities for opera'. Britten did not want a compromise; if opera worked, it would be a bonus, but his priority was 'a concert hall, with a concert hall acoustic', and seating for between 700 and 800. Meanwhile, the building was to be kept, both inside and out, in sympathy with the Victorian industrial buildings at Snape.

Britten's record company, Decca, gave a ten-year covenant – Britten planned to use the new hall as his personal recording studio – and the new hall was to be wired for the BBC to record during the Festival. An appeal was

Snape Maltings in 1966, before the conversion. The photograph was taken by John Brandenburger of Arup Associates, principal architect for the Concert Hall project

LEFT: The original roof being dismantled. Arup designed a steeper roof, a slope of 45 degrees, to help with the acoustics, and the original bluffs were replaced with replicas, but serving the same purpose of ventilation

ABOVE: Pumping water out of the orchestra pit

launched to raise the necessary funds – 'by far the greatest undertaking we have attempted', Britten admitted in a personal letter to the Queen. In May 1966, a 25-year lease was signed (later increased to 99 years), and demolition began, with Wm. C. Reade of Aldeburgh appointed as the main contractor and Bill Muttitt as foreman.

The New House (Kiln No. 5) contained four drying kilns, with eight large furnaces below. The existing roof, recalled Derek Sugden, had become virtually charcoal. The inner walls, the brick hoppers and the suspended drying floors were removed, together with the original roof. Excavations showed a lack of suitable foundations, so considerable underpinning was also necessary.

At one end was to be the stage, spanning the full width of the new space, some 40 feet (12m) deep and four feet (1.2m) high. The interior layout of the auditorium was dictated partly by the needs of Decca for recording. They wanted a further 30 feet of flat area in front of the stage before the start of the raked seating. The raked area provided space beneath for plant and for the public toilet facilities, giving onto a foyer that ran along the length of the Hall. The adjacent two-storeyed building, now behind the stage, was a natural place for dressing rooms at ground-floor level and a restaurant on the first floor, offering wonderful views to the east across the marshes.

In his article in the *Arup Journal* of June 1967, Derek Sugden writes that the roof design was key to the whole conversion. While wanting to keep the shape of the original structure, they also wanted as much height as possible, and a 45° slope was chosen, with a flat top to support the four ventilators, which copied the old chimney bluffs and each weighed some 2.5 tons. Once the inner walls were removed, it was found that the width of the newly created hall varied by as much as 18 inches (approx. 46 cm). The original walls were raised by two feet (0.6 metre), using the old red bricks, made in Snape and rescued from the demolition of the interior walls. The main walls were then stiffened with piers and arches made from new Aldeburgh bricks, and a reinforced concrete beam. On the rear wall of the auditorium a cantilevered lighting box was constructed, following the design of the traditional lucams – white timber-clad projections from the roof, containing a winch – seen elsewhere on the site.

The whole of the area below the stage was excavated to a depth of 4ft 6in (1.4m) below that of the auditorium to allow space for access, an extension of the orchestra pit, and for traps in the stage. The low-lying level of the building meant that water started seeping into the pit as it was being dug, and pumps had to work day and night to keep water at bay while the concrete shell dried (a pump is still in situ to cope with any further water ingress following high tides). The stage, made of 1¼- inch gurjun hardwood strip, is flat, but has jacks beneath, operated by a two-hp motor, to allow it to be raked for dramatic productions.

In order to maintain the character of the building, finishings were kept to a minimum. The timber is untreated, the walls grit-blasted and sealed, and the steelwork left in its original finish. Richard Butt of the BBC suggested that the seating should be made out of cane, similar to that originally used at Wagner's Festival Theatre in Bayreuth. Imogen Holst is reported to have declared that the chairs 'mustn't be too comfortable! ... They should make people sit properly ... they should be able to sit up straight!'. The 830 cane and ash seats cost £6 4s. 3d. each and were made in Ipswich by Wrinch and Sons Ltd. They have been maintained ever since by a local craftsman, George Cook.

In acoustic tests in front of an invited audience, the reverberation time proved to be 'bang on two seconds': exactly on target. The volume of space in the Hall created by the height of the roof – some 288,800 cubic feet – together with the hardness of the brick walls, baked over so many years, plus the lack of soft furnishings, all contributed to the perfection of the acoustic.

Snape Maltings Concert Hall was officially opened by H.M. Queen Elizabeth II on Friday 2 June 1967. She arrived at Bentwaters Airbase at noon, and after a visit to Aldeburgh's Moot Hall and to Britten's home at the Red House, she arrived at Snape to a fanfare and the waving of Union Jacks. George Gooderham's daughter, Mary-Jane, presented the Queen with a bouquet, and Britten handed her the keys to the Hall.

In her speech, the Queen said: 'Starting on a small scale, and perhaps partly as an act of faith, you have built up a festival and you have encouraged the arts to flower in the soil of this pleasant part of Suffolk. The news of your success has spread far and wide in Britain and beyond our shores. I congratulate you and the architect and the builders and I have much pleasure in declaring open the Maltings Concert Hall and Opera House.'

The royal party sat in Row L. The opening work in the first concert – following Britten's own arrangement of the National Anthem – was Britten's Op.79, *The Building of the House*, specially composed for the occasion, sung by a chorus comprised of amateur choirs from all over East Anglia. Britten wrote in the programme: 'I wrote this true example of Occasional Music during December and January of the past winter. It was certainly inspired by the excitement of the planning and building – and the haste!' That the first piece in the programme should involve an amateur choir again demonstrated Britten's commitment that the Festival should involve the community.

Queen Elizabeth II opens Snape Maltings Concert Hall on 2 June 1967, as Prince Philip and Benjamin Britten look on

The completed Snape
Maltings Concert Hall

The Concert Hall's ability to be turned into an opera house was tested on the following Wednesday, when the Royal Opera House, Covent Garden, presented a new production of Britten's *A Midsummer Night's Dream*. In the final week of the Festival, there was even a programme of dance on the new stage, when the Harlow Ballet Club performed to the music of Monteverdi.

William Mann wrote in the *Times* (9 June 1967) 'The acoustics ... are so beautiful, the furnishings so favourable, the size so right, that this hall seems to promise as rosily developing a future for music as did John Christie's Glyndebourne Opera House in 1934.' *The Financial Times* called it 'the best concert hall we have. It is a brilliant refashioning', while the local newspaper, the *East Anglian Daily Times*, referred to its location as 'a stroke of genius'. For the *Sunday Times* it was 'in every way a resounding success'.

There was a concern that with the move to Snape the nature and atmosphere of the Festival would change, but it was determined from the start that the vital links with Aldeburgh would be maintained. The Jubilee Hall would remain the Festival's opera house, and concerts would continue to be performed in local churches. But from this point, major concerts in the Festival would be performed at the new concert hall, where for the first time over 800 people could enjoy a performance, in a perfect acoustic. Ticket sales for the Festival rose from 14,650 in the previous year, to 34,800, with concerts playing to virtually 100 per cent of capacity, a great boost to the Festival's finances.

George Ewart Evans summed up the mood of optimism that accompanied the opening of the Concert Hall as a venue for the Aldeburgh Festival: 'The move to Snape can only bring about a deepening and strengthening of the Festival's indigenous character. Nor could another spot have been chosen that so much enshrines the atmosphere or ambience of the Aldeburgh Festival. For the Malt House is within a stone's throw of the river; and from its east side there is a remarkably fine view of the heath, marshland and estuary which – along with the grey, silver-flecked Aldeburgh sea – are the Festival's continuing undersong, the inspiration it grew from and still draws upon for much of its artistic sustenance.'

All seemed set for a great new chapter in the history of the Aldeburgh Festival.

TOP: Detail of the roof, showing the rafters made of douglas fir, and the ties in 1-inch diameter high tensile steel with bottle screws

CENTRE: The Festival artistic directors pose outside their new Concert Hall, 1969

BELOW: The completed Concert Hall

CHAPTER 6
The Fire and After

The 22nd Aldeburgh Festival opened on 7 June 1969 with an afternoon recital at the Concert Hall. Benjamin Britten joined the Amadeus Quartet for a programme including Schubert's 'Trout' Quintet, playing his own Steinway piano. After the concert, the Festival audience moved back to Aldeburgh for an 8.30pm performance of two new one-act operas by Gordon Crosse at the Jubilee Hall. While Festival audiences were enjoying Crosse's *Purgatory* and *The Grace of Todd*, events back at Snape were to take a tragic turn.

Oscar 'Ordy' Rumsey, former maltster and now caretaker of the Concert Hall, made the building secure at around 8pm. Later that evening, several people noticed the sky turning red, as flames took hold of the roof of the Hall.

Doris Ling – later to work at the Hall with her husband, ex-maltster Bob – was living on the Terrace in the village. She described going outside to watch the drama unfolding down the hill below: 'What a sight that was! All those flames – just as though the heat lifted the roof, because it seemed to be suspended in the air above the flames, and then it went down again. That was the illusion from where we were. There were crowds watching from the terrace and when they heard the snapping they thought it was whisky-bottles exploding, not realizing it was the asbestos slates on the roof going bang, bang, bang!'

Anne Gibson of Street Farm, Snape, told a newspaper reporter,: 'The fire took only seconds to sweep the roof of the Concert Hall from end to end'. Pat Lord, who was in a full Plough and Sail playing cards that evening, said that most people were in shock. The fire service came from Saxmundham with 60 firemen, and had the blaze under control in less than two hours; fortunately, the direction of the wind meant that no further buildings were

After the opening performance of the 1969 Aldeburgh Festival, the Concert Hall caught fire

LEFT: The day after the fire revealed the full extent of the damage to the Hall

ABOVE: One of the main casualties of the fire was Britten's own Steinway piano, which he had last played only hours before

BELOW: Britten, followed by news cameramen, surveying the damage to the stage

Rosamund Strode, Britten's assistant, captured this photograph of the contractors rebuilding the roof trusses during the restoration following the fire

damaged. But with so much wood to fuel the flames, only the brick shell of the Hall remained, along with the twisted ruins of Britten's Steinway: 'it was the nicest piano I ever played on,' Britten mourned the following day.

Graham Nicholson, who was spending his university vacation as a general driver for Britten and Pears, remembers hearing about the fire on the early morning radio news. 'I thought I should go straight down to the Red House – I think I must have been there by 9 o'clock if not before – and Ben had just come off the phone to the Bishop [of St Edmundsbury and Ipswich]. There had already been a summit meeting, and it had been decided that the "Festival must go on," and the Bishop had given permission that concerts programmed for the Concert Hall could be relocated to Blythburgh Church. We went up to Snape in Ben's Alvis, and wandered around the smouldering, burnt-out ruin of the Concert Hall. There was a mixture of shock, and huge disappointment, but a quiet resolution that the Concert Hall would be rebuilt.'

Under the headline, 'Ashes of a Dream', the local paper quoted Britten: 'I cannot describe my emotions and feelings ... My first reaction was one of shock and desperation, and a feeling that we had better go away and forget all about the festival for a week or two. But this was followed immediately by a determination that the festival must go on.' The Queen Mother rang Britten personally to express her condolences, and sympathies were offered in Parliament "at the loss of this fine building".

Immediate plans were put in place to find alternative venues for the 17 remaining concerts scheduled to take place at Snape; the main opera production – Handel's *Idomeneo* to be conducted by Britten and with Pears in the leading role – was relocated to Blythburgh Church, with replacement costumes loaned from the Royal Opera House. Only one concert was cancelled as a result of the fire, although there was naturally disappointment at the reduced seating capacity for many of the concerts.

There were conflicting stories about how the fire started; could it have been a discarded cigarette, or an electrical fault? There was some controversy surrounding the inadequate fire precautions that had been allowed. Fortunately, the design of the roof and the buttressing of the walls meant that the structure of the Concert Hall was still sound, and the foyer, restaurant and dressing rooms were largely unscathed. Plans were immediately put

Britten and Prudence, Lady Penn with a model of the Snape Maltings Concert Hall, 14 May 1970. Lady Penn was one of a small committee who helped raise funds for the rebuiling of the Hall. Britten is pointing at the building that became the Britten Studio in 2009

into place to resurrect the Hall, and clearance of the debris began on 30 June. It was to be rebuilt largely to the original plan, but with significantly enhanced fire protection, along with some other technical improvements such as a lift to raise and lower the forestage to create the orchestra pit, improved wiring and lighting and the extension of scenery stores, rehearsal space and dressing rooms. During the works, the grass terrace had to be extended and fortified against high water following the highest-ever breakthrough of the river wall in September – 'the new menace'. Ironically, the fire took place only hours after it had been announced that, after four years of intensive fund-raising, the £176,000 cost of converting the Concert Hall had been met. However, the Hall was fully insured (through Sun Alliance), and many artists appearing in the Festival that year donated their fees to the Snape Maltings Rebuilding Fund, set up to raise an additional sum to cover the costs of the improvements. A concert tour to the USA with Britten and Pears had in any event been planned for that autumn to continue the fund-raising programme, and this now helped to augment the rebuilding fund.

The Concert Hall was rebuilt in 42 weeks, at a cost of £225,000. The opening concert of the 23rd Aldeburgh Festival on 5 June 1970 was once again attended by H.M. the Queen, although this time there was no formal re-opening.

Three days later, a year after its original scheduled appearance, *Idomeneo* was finally staged at Snape Maltings.

CHAPTER 7

The Aldeburgh Festival at Snape

While many events still took place in Aldeburgh, the new Concert Hall at Snape, with its greatly enhanced stage and audience capacity, offered the Aldeburgh Festival the opportunity to expand both its programme, and its audience. There was an enhanced level of comfort for both artists and attenders, and while at first people may have missed the walk along the beach during the interval, they were soon won over by the incomparable views across the marshes.

Larger-scale orchestral works could now be presented at the Festival, which now had two more artistic directors, Philip Ledger and Colin Graham. In 1970, Shostakovich's 14th Symphony – dedicated to Britten – had its first performance outside the USSR at Snape Maltings. For many years, Simon Rattle brought his City of Birmingham Symphony Orchestra to Snape. A strong connection with Russian music continued: Rostropovich and Richter were frequent visitors, Boris Christoff sang in a recital in 1973, and Shostakovich's Viola Sonata was premiered in 1976.

Although not designed for opera, the Concert Hall proved very capable of being turned into an opera stage. The Royal Opera presented Britten's *A Midsummer Night's Dream* in the opening season, and on 16 June 1973, the first performance of Britten's final opera, *Death in Venice*, was given at the Concert Hall, with Pears in the role of Aschenbach. Britten himself could not be at the premiere as he was seriously ill at the time. A special performance was given two months later for him to see it for the first time. A new production of *Albert Herring* was mounted the following year, with Anthony Rolfe Johnson as Albert and Thomas Allen in the role of Sid. Rolfe Johnson recalled that on the morning of the first performance he was summoned to the Red House to go through the part with the composer. At the end of the session, Britten said, 'Very nice, my dear, but I do wish you'd sing what I wrote.'

The Concert Hall was not just used for larger-scale works; the Hall was equally effective as a setting for more intimate solo performances, and Pears, with Britten accompanying, gave many recitals on the Concert

Queen Elizabeth the Queen Mother was a frequent visitor to Snape, and became the Festival's patron

ABOVE: Britten's opera *Death in Venice* had its premiere at Snape Maltings Concert Hall in 1973. Peter Pears played Aschenbach, but Britten was too ill to attend

ABOVE LEFT: The Britten–Pears Young Artist Programme revived *Death in Venice* for the 2007 Festival

LEFT: Janet Baker, Britten and Steuart Bedford rehearse *Phaedra* in 1976

Hall stage. Britten would frequently feature both on the keyboard and on the podium. Marion Thorpe recalled a performance of the Mozart Requiem, conducted by Britten at Snape in 1971: 'It was a performance of almost uncanny intensity and insight into the music – as though somehow Ben himself was creating the work there and then.' She speaks of the awe in which audiences were held by his mesmeric performances, despite an apparently considerable lack of self-confidence on his own part.

In contrast, John Dankworth and Cleo Laine, Joyce Grenfell, Peggy Ashcroft and actors from the Royal Shakespeare Company made regular appearances; Princess Grace of Monaco took part in a poetry recital in 1978.

In 1976, in what was to be Britten's last Festival, Janet Baker sang the premiere of his dramatic cantata *Phaedra* in a Festival that also included performances by André Previn, Elizabeth Söderström, Richter and the entire Rostropovich family.

After the death of Britten in 1976, Pears continued to lead the Festival's artistic planning, in association with a variety of other artists – Mstislav Rostropovich, Murray Perahia, Simon Rattle, John Shirley-Quirk – until his own death ten years later. Steuart Bedford, who had known Britten since he was a child and had conducted the premiere of *Death in Venice* in 1973, joined the team of artistic directors in 1974. He was artistic director of the Festival for 25 years. He returned to Snape to conduct *Peter Grimes* in the Britten centenary Festival, 2013.

After Pears's death, the two estates were constituted into the Britten–Pears Foundation, with the objects of supporting the Aldeburgh Festival, maintaining the Britten–Pears Library, archive, and the Red House, and to promote music by Britten, particularly that which had hitherto been unheard or withdrawn. Chairman of the Britten Estate and music director of the Britten–Pears Foundation, composer Colin Matthews, worked for Britten on *Death in Venice*, making the vocal score from his sketches, and filling in orchestral parts. Premieres of his own works have frequently been given at the Festival, and he was guest artistic associate for the centenary year Festival in 2013.

In 1998, Jonathan Reekie joined as chief executive of what is now called Aldeburgh Music, and placed new opera back at the centre of the Festival. When Thomas Adès became sole artistic director in 1999, his first Festival was launched with a new production of his own opera, *Powder Her Face*. In 2009 the first performance of Harrison Birtwistle's scena for soprano, tenor and six instruments, *The Corridor*, helped to launch the new Britten Studio.

Elizabeth Söderström, a guest artistic director of the Aldeburgh Festival in 1990, wrote that 'Through the years Aldeburgh has succeeded in "keeping alive a tradition of innovation"… Thanks to devoted friends and skilful management there is perfection and joy.' That remains true to this day.

The Aldeburgh Festival continues to inspire and surprise audiences with its mix of old and new, and Snape Maltings Concert Hall remains the vibrant centre of a programme that constantly challenges perceptions and breaks new ground. The performance spaces within the Hoffmann Building, opened in 2009, have created informal places where initiatives such as Faster than Sound, which explores connections between classical music and new media, can sit alongside the varied programme that regularly fills an 800-seat concert hall in the middle of rural Suffolk.

LEFT: Simon Rattle, once a member of the Festival's artistic directorate, conducting the City of Birmingham Symphony Orchestra and mezzo soprano Magdalena Kožená in *Das Lied von der Erde* during the 2011 Festival

BELOW LEFT: Jonathan Reekie, who became Aldeburgh Music's chief executive in 1998

BELOW RIGHT: Composer Colin Matthews has a long association with Britten's music and the Festival

ABOVE LEFT: Composer and conductor Oliver Knussen, one of the artistic directorate following Britten's death, who still regularly appears in the Festival

ABOVE RIGHT: Composer, conductor and pianist Thomas Adès was artistic director of the Aldeburgh Festival from 1999 to 2008

LEFT: Of the many artists who managed to sell out their concerts at the Hall, few were able to attract a full house as quickly as pianist Alfred Brendel

BELOW: Pianist Pierre-Laurent Aimard became the Festival's artistic director in 2009. Here he talks to composer Elliott Carter, a number of whose works were premiered at the Festival

CHAPTER 8

Nurturing Talent

As early as 1953, Britten and Pears, both committed to the musical development of young people, formed the idea of having a music school attached to the Aldeburgh Festival. The fundamental concept was 'to prepare and promote young singers or string players for professional life at the very highest level'. The first masterclasses, which took place over the course of a weekend and were led by Pears, with Graham Johnson as accompanist, were given in September 1972. The next year, the experiment was repeated, with Roger Vignoles and the 18-year-old Simon Rattle also engaged as accompanists. By 1974, there was a fortnight-long course for singers. Plans were set in train for a programme of string studies, and in 1975 a Snape Maltings Training Orchestra, formed by Cecil Aronowitz, and later to become the Britten–Pears Orchestra, rehearsed and performed in the Hall for the first time. By the time of Britten's death in 1976, the programme had expanded to six courses, including cello masterclasses with Mstislav Rostropovich.

In order to create a dedicated space where this training could take place, the Benjamin Britten Memorial Appeal was launched, and the barley store adjacent to the Concert Hall was converted by Arup Associates into a home for what is now known as the Britten–Pears Young Artist Programme.

Opened on 28 April 1979 by the patron of the then Aldeburgh Foundation, H.M. Queen Elizabeth the Queen Mother, in the presence of the newly knighted Peter Pears, the School incorporated a 114-seat recital room (now named after Pears) and a top-floor seminar room, with many practice rooms in between. The Holst Library, holding Imogen Holst's collection of manuscripts and music books, remains an invaluable resource for students. From the windows, one can look out over the marshes towards the river, and over the same landscape that inspired Britten and his contemporaries.

The barley store, shown in the 1970s before its conversion

ABOVE: The Britten–Pears Building, the home of the Britten–Pears Young Artist Programme

LEFT: Practice room at the Britten–Pears Building

BELOW: A 114-seat Recital Room provides the Britten–Pears students with a high-quality rehearsal and performance space. It is now called the Peter Pears Recital Room

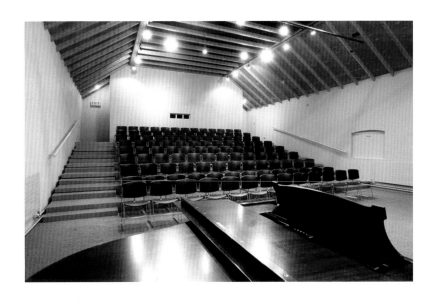

Peter Pears teaching soprano
Lynne Dawson, 1981

In 1979, Rostropovich conducted the Britten–Pears School in a performance of *Eugene Onegin* (with Pears and Eric Crozier as guest artists in the roles of M. Triquet and the valet Guillot). In subsequent years, the School regularly performed an opera during the Festival.

Artist development remains at the heart of the Aldeburgh philosophy. The 'School' was re-named the Britten–Pears Young Artist Programme in 2003, and has grown into the largest programme in the UK for developing the talents of emerging professional musicians. The aim remains as it has been from the beginning to bridge formal musical education and the professional life, exposing developing artists in a safe and nurturing environment to the life of the performer through encounters with the skills and talents of world-class artists and teachers. Over the years, such leading artists as Joan Sutherland, Ann Murray, Thomas Allen, Galina Vishnevskaya, Murray Perahia, Charles Mackerras, Rostropovich and Elisabeth Söderström, as well as Pears himself, have been notable teachers, while its many alumni have included Thomas Adès, Ian Bostridge, Simon Keenlyside and Felicity Lott, some of whom now return to teach as well.

Since the very first course in 1972, over 10,000 young artists have attended the Britten–Pears Programme, and many have gone on to become leading musicians in their own right. Auditions are held across the world, now using the internet to access countries on the other side of the globe.

To coincide with London 2012 and the Olympic Games in London, the Aldeburgh World Orchestra was formed. Conducted by Mark Elder, it brought together 124 exceptional young musicians from 35 countries. In that year, the AWO performed both at Snape and as part of the BBC Proms at the Royal Albert Hall, as well as on a short European tour.

A logical extension to the Britten–Pears Young Artist Programme was Aldeburgh Residencies, launched in 2003. Established musicians had long looked on the opportunities afforded to young artists with some envy, lamenting the lack of development opportunities available for the working artist. With seed funding from Arts Council England, Aldeburgh Music was able to create bespoke opportunities for artists who wanted to take time out of their busy lives to come to Suffolk, to create new repertoire, make new connections and develop new partnerships away from the pressure of their performance schedule. The Residencies were an instant success.

Snape provides an inspirational environment for the training of young musicians

Aldeburgh Education was officially created in 1991, although Britten had started working with young people in the first Aldeburgh Festival back in 1948, with the aim of breaking down barriers between the amateur and the professional. The first annual Celebration of Schools' Music took place at the Concert Hall in 1987, when, with support from Suffolk County Council, schools from all over the county were invited to present some of their work in the prestigious setting of the Concert Hall stage. For many young people, it was their first experience of performing in front of a large audience, and remains a fond memory and inspiration. The work of Aldeburgh Education, however, has developed far beyond just working with schools and colleges, to encompass annual community performances and work with juvenile offenders at HMP and YOI Warren Hill, using modern technology to engage with youngsters of all abilities and from all backgrounds.

To support younger musicians, Aldeburgh Young Musicians was launched for children of exceptional potential from the Eastern region, from the age of eight years upwards. It provides advanced music mentoring for gifted young musicians, with intensive residential activity over school holidays and weekends.

Most of these initiatives to support emerging talent result in public performances, and the public is encouraged to attend the masterclasses and recitals. And even during rehearsals, as visitors wander round the Maltings site with their shopping bags or exercising their dogs, there are innumerable public encounters with young musicians carrying their instruments, or the sound of song or strings pouring forth from the open windows of the practice rooms, all part of the musical 'Snape experience'.

CHAPTER 9

Fulfilling Britten's Vision

In the spring of 1970, Britten and Pears commissioned a masterplan from Arup Associates that would turn some of the redundant buildings adjacent to the Concert Hall into an 'Arts Centre'. But with the lack of the necessary financial resources, the plans remained a dream. Once Britten died in 1976 the plans, beyond the conversion of the granary store into the Britten–Pears School in 1979, lay dormant.

When the Concert Hall was originally opened, it was solely for the annual Aldeburgh Festival – no more than three weeks each June. However, with its marvelous acoustic and inspirational location, it soon became the venue for a much more extended programme of performance and other activity. By 1969, the Hall was already being used as a regular venue for the BBC series 'Jazz at the Maltings', and was turned into a studio for the BBC TV film of *Peter Grimes*. The improved recording facilities following the restoration after the fire made it a popular venue for sound recordings, while the largest stage in East Anglia made it a perfect setting for ballet and dance.

Short seasons of concerts began to be programmed for the summer and autumn. In 1982, the August Snape Proms was launched – it was at first a long weekend of five wildly varying concerts, ranging from jazz trumpeter and bandleader Humphrey Lyttelton to a Viennese evening. For three years from 1983, Rostropovich directed a festival at the start of August. By 1988 the month-long Snape Proms that we know today became an established part of the calendar. Major musical events were also presented each year at Easter and in the autumn. The annual Celebration of Schools' Music, along with dance, opera and other musical events and regular use by community groups, came to fill the Hall's schedule. For 340 days from 1983 to 1985, the Concert Hall was used as the venue for the Sizewell B enquiry.

In 1999, architects Penoyre and Prasad designed a new restaurant above the Oyster Bar, raising the roof to provide exciting views across the marshes

By 1996, it was felt that the Concert Hall was at a turning point; there was a pressing need to improve levels of comfort and accessibility, to update and augment facilities for public, artists and staff alike in a building that had now been open for almost half a century. A 50th anniversary appeal was launched and the sums raised enabled the construction of the new outer foyer (in time for the 50th Festival in 1997) and to designs by Penoyre and Prasad, the expansion of the public areas and the redesign of the restaurant, with its magnificent view across the reedbeds. By the opening night of the 1999 Festival there was also a new terrace, funded by donations from the Friends of Aldeburgh Music; new education and exhibition facilities; enlarged dressing rooms, improved facilities for artists and technical improvements, including a new moveable lighting grid.

In the early 1980s, the industrial operation of Gooderham and Hayward's animal feed business – which had been operating 24-hour shifts making milk powder alongside activities at the Concert Hall throughout the 1970s – had wound down. The Gooderham family had developed the commercial side of the Maltings, initially with the Craft Shop in 1971, and then with the conversion of the large barley silo into the House & Garden store in 1991. However, at the start of the new century some 60 per cent of the buildings on the site remained unused, and were, in the words of Johnny Gooderham, 'showing signs of significant fatigue'. Initially, the local authority had wanted the Gooderham family to continue to develop the Grade II-listed site with further light industry, but the economics did not make sense. The owners saw the future of the Maltings in year-round tourism, residential and destination retail, with the extension in 1997 of the flagship House & Garden.

Meanwhile, with the further expansion of Aldeburgh Music under chief executive Jonathan Reekie – the continuing success of the Britten–Pears Young Artist Programme, the formation of Aldeburgh Residencies, the creation of Aldeburgh Young Musicians and the expanding performance programme – pressure was put on the existing music facilities at Snape.

One morning in the windy autumn of 2004, staff arriving after a stormy night saw that irreversible damage had been caused to some of the unused derelict buildings adjacent to the Concert Hall. This galvanized both Aldeburgh Music and the Gooderham family to work together, with encouragement from Suffolk Coastal District Council, on a masterplan, to conserve once and for all the remaining buildings on the Maltings site.

With funding from the Arts Council Lottery, a new foyer was added in 1999, which provided much needed circulation space for audiences

LEFT: Many of the original maltings buildings remained unused and semi-derelict, even into the new century

BELOW: By May 2007, work was underway on the foyer of the new building

Arts Council England and the local authorities were very supportive of the idea of expanding facilities at Snape to create a major music campus for Aldeburgh Music, that would be unique in Europe. Negotiations to buy a new 999-year lease from the Gooderham family and an Arts Council and a Lottery grant kick-started the project.

A new campus was to be created from the redundant and semi-derelict kilns and granaries adjacent to the Concert Hall, acquired from the Gooderhams. These buildings had been identified by Britten and Pears as long ago as the early 1970s as ripe for conversion to create their longed-for Arts Centre. Haworth Tompkins was appointed architect for the project. What Arup Associates achieved in 1967 – creating a new space while preserving the original building's history and atmosphere – they were to accomplish in 2009.

The Hoffmann Building was opened in May 2009. A high-ceilinged foyer converted from one of the silos leads to the centrepiece of the new complex, the Britten Studio. This created Snape's first dedicated rehearsal space large enough to accommodate a symphony orchestra, but with flexible seating to turn it into a 340-seat auditorium. The roof is similar in shape to that of the original Concert Hall (although seven times heavier, in order to create recording-standard sound insulation), with retractable absorbent banners that can adjust the reverberation time as required. Other features to ensure a perfect acoustic include timber bass-absorbency panels, fixed with timber wedges, at the upper part of the auditorium walls, with a lower section inspired by Aldeburgh beach – its mix of hard and uneven surfaces designed to dissipate sound reflection as easily as possible.

On the upper level is a converted kiln – the Jerwood Kiln Studio – that can seat up to 80 and provides suitable rehearsal or performance space for a chamber group or soloist. The roof of this double-height studio is clad with blackened timbers, many salvaged from the old kilns during the dismantling process.

Back downstairs are two further studios that double as rehearsal spaces and dressing rooms – the Foyle and Weinrebe studios. A former granary, with its original trussed timber roof, now houses new office accommodation, and the mezzanine lounge area – known as the Bakery in honour of the mezzo-soprano Janet Baker, who has long been associated with Britten and Aldeburgh – provides a common space for artists and audience to sit and relax. Many of the original features in the Hoffmann Building have been retained – such as an upside-down granary door and the original Garrett-produced bosses – with the additional timber and brickwork chosen to blend in with the original structure.

TOP: The original kiln and storage barns adjacent to the Concert Hall were identified by Britten as potentially suitable for conversion into a studio as early as the 1970s

CENTRE: The Hoffmann Building, designed by Haworth Tompkins and opened in 2009

BELOW LEFT: At the heart of the Hoffmann Building is the Britten Studio

BELOW RIGHT: The roof design reflects that of the original Concert Hall but is seven times heavier

TOP: Inside the Hoffmann Building, the foyer retains the atmosphere of an industrial building

CENTRE: The Victorian dovecote has been brought back to life as a small studio with a wonderful view over the marshes beyond

BELOW: The Britten–Pears Building has been given new access, and also contains the Trask Artists' Cafe, a new meeting place for artists working at Snape

The Pumphouse, located on the edge of the
marshes in Aldeburgh, provides an atmospheric
small space for fringe events during the Festival

The remains of the Victorian dovecote, long disintegrated, now incorporate a small standalone studio, a box made of self-weathering corten steel. The new building has outstanding views across the marshes and is an inspirational space for a composer or writer in which to work. The 1979 Britten–Pears School building has been renovated and given a more accessible entrance, and a link to the new Trask Artists' Café – a meeting place for staff and artists. The Pond Gallery has been reconfigured, and a new visitor centre, shop and box office has been created. Elsewhere on the site, the Gooderham family has further developed its commercial activity, with the aim of finally bringing all the Victorian industrial buildings into 21st-century use.

Meanwhile back in Aldeburgh, a former Victorian Pumphouse on the edges of the marshes was donated to Aldeburgh Music. Dubbed a 'mini-Maltings', its 60-seat capacity makes it an ideal venue for fringe performances during the Festival.

This part of the Suffolk coast – once a quiet backwater that largely earned its living from the sea – was transformed in the 19th century by a far-sighted entrepreneur, who saw the potential of a site by the river to develop his malting business, and become one of the most successful industrial concerns in East Anglia. A century later, an equally visionary musician saw the potential of the site for a new and original purpose. And in the 21st century, Snape, Aldeburgh and the Suffolk coast have, as a result of the heritage laid down by these two inspirational people, become synonymous with music and the development of world-class musicianship.

With music breathing new life into the Victorian brickwork, a new chapter in the rich history of this beautiful part of East Anglia is just beginning.

AFTERWORD
Sculpture at Snape

From the beginning, the Aldeburgh Festival was of Music 'and the Arts', and the visual arts have always featured as part of the annual Festival programme – triggered by Peter Pears, who was a great art collector.

Benjamin Britten and Henry Moore had known each other since the 1940s, and had occasionally worked on the same projects, and for the same patrons. They were appointed to the Order of Merit within two years of each other, and Moore donated a small bronze to the Aldeburgh Foundation's appeal to renovate and improve the Jubilee Hall. For the opening of the Concert Hall in 1967, Moore was also persuaded to loan his *Working Model for Reclining Figure* (Lincoln Center), situated on a platform in front of the main entrance. From 1971 to 2005, Henry Moore and, after his death, the Henry Moore Foundation, continued to loan bronzes for the lawn in front of the Concert Hall. In 2005, *Reclining Figure* was removed by the Foundation to feature in an exhibition elsewhere, and for a number of years, the site was occupied by works by a variety of contemporary artists, including Damien Hirst, Sarah Lucas and Angus Fairhurst. In 2012, a Henry Moore returned to the lawn when his *Large Interior Form* (1981–2) was installed on loan.

Britten and Pears were also friends with Barbara Hepworth, and in 1976 three pieces from her *Family of Man* (1970) were erected on the lawn next to the reedbed. They are on permanent loan from the Fitzwilliam Museum, Cambridge, in accordance with her will.

The front of the Concert Hall has been the setting for a sculpture by Henry Moore for many years. This is *Large Interior Form* (1981–2), installed in the autumn of 2011

TOP: Barbara Hepworth's *Family of Man* (1970) is set on a lawn across from the Concert Hall

LEFT: Hepworth's *Family of Man* dominates and yet blends with the natural landscape

TOP: The imposing *Perceval* (2006) by Sarah Lucas was installed in an adjacent field in 2010

LEFT: Alison Wilding's *Migrant* (2003) – 'a glimpse of bird and boat', according to its creator

In the ditch leading to the sluice gate, is Alison Wilding's *Migrant* (2003). '*Migrant* is about travelling, not destination,' says Wilding; 'Its nature is changeable, secretive – a glimpse of bird and boat.'

From 2010, *Perceval* (2006) by Sarah Lucas has been sited in an adjoining field. A monumental painted bronze shire-horse and cart laden with giant concrete marrows looks real from a distance, yet close-up is playfully similar to a kitsch mantelpiece ornament.

Temporary exhibitions have always been held in the Concert Hall Gallery, in the Peter Pears Gallery in Aldeburgh, and more recently at the Pond Gallery at Snape Maltings. At the Aldeburgh Festival in 2011, a major new initiative was launched with SNAP, a show of living artists with links to the region, brought together by Sadie Coles, Sarah Lucas and Abigail Lane. SNAP used not only the Hall but the lawns, external sites and disused outbuildings within the complex to show a diverse selection of sculpture, photography, drawing, moving images and sound.

The inner foyer of the Concert Hall is dominated by the lifesize figure of a bull by the sculptor Georg Ehrlich (1897–1966). The bronze was presented to Britten and Pears by the lifelong patron of the Festival, the Princess Margaret of Hesse and the Rhine, on the occasion of the re-opening of the Hall after the fire. Ehrlich, a close friend of Britten and Pears, also sculpted the two busts of Britten (1951) and Pears (1963) that are in the Visitor Centre.

On the upper foyer level sits *Apollo*, carved in white Italian marble by John Skeaping RA (1901–1980). The sculpture was created in Italy in 1925, the same year of Skeaping's marriage to Barbara Hepworth, and was given in memory of Britten by Peter and Mollie du Sautoy in 1978, in the second year after the composer's death.

The bronze bust on a pedestal at the top of the foyer stairs is of Fidelity, Countess of Cranbrook, the first Chairman of the Aldeburgh Festival. It is by Frances Baruch FRBS, and is dated 1982.

The painting on the stairs is of Imogen Holst (1907–1984), composer and one-time artistic director of the Aldeburgh Festival. Imogen Holst sat for the painting, by Mary Potter (1900–1981), in 1954.

CONCERT HALL FOYER SCULPTURES: *Peter Pears* (1963) by Georg Ehrlich; *Benjamin Britten* (1951), by Georg Ehrlich; *Bull*, by Georg Ehrlich; *Fidelity, Countess of Cranbrook* (1982), by Frances Baruch

Sources and Acknowledgements

Sources

Bennett, Moira *Making Musicians: A Personal History of the Britten–Pears School* (The Bittern Press, 2012), extract in Aldeburgh Festival programme book 2012

Carpenter, Humphrey *Benjamin Britten* (1992)

Crabbe, George *Tales 1812*

Crabbe, George *The Life of George Crabbe by his Son* (The Cresset Press Ltd, 1947)

Crozier, Eric *Talking with Bob and Doris: Reflections of East Suffolk Life* (1987)

Grogan, Christopher, ed. *Imogen Holst: A Life in Music* (2007)

Headington, Christopher *Britten* (1996)

Holst, Imogen *Britten* (1966)

Hughes, Diana *Aldeburgh Revisited* (The Aldeburgh Museum in association with The Aldeburgh Bookshop, 2008)

Irving, Ruth *Snape*, (1945, rev.1966)

Jebb, Miles, ed. *East Anglia: An Anthology* (Barrie and Jenkins, 1990)

Palmer, Tony, dir. *A Time There Was* (BBC documentary, 1980)

Paye, Peter *The Snape Branch* (Oakwood Press, 2005)

Paye, Peter *The Aldeburgh Branch* (Oakwood Press, 2012)

Pipe, Julia *Port on the Alde* (1976, rev.1999)

Redstone, Vincent B. *Memorials of Old Suffolk* (undated, Suffolk Record Office)

Reekie, Jonathan and Banks, Ariane, ed. *New Aldeburgh Anthology* (Boydell Press, 2009)

Reeve, Stanley *Stanley Reeve Recalls* (1995)

Simper, Robert *Over Snape Bridge* (1967)

Sugden, Derek 'Snape Concert Hall', *The Arup Journal*, Vol.2 No.4, (June 1967)

Tompkins, Steve 'Listening to the Maltings', Housewarming programme book (2009), repr. 62nd Aldeburgh Festival programme book (2009)

Waddell, John 'Snape', from website www.snapevillage.info

Wake-Walker, Jenni, ed. *Time and Concord: Aldeburgh Festival Recollections* (1997)

Aldeburgh Festival Programme Books 1948–present

Soundings magazine

www.aldeburghmuseumonline.co.uk (for the history of Aldeburgh)

www.wikitree.com (for details of the Garrett estate)

Illustration and photo credits

The author is extremely grateful to the following for allowing their images to be used in this book:

Reproduced by permission of Aldeburgh Museum Trust **7, 9**
The late Dr. Ian Allen, reproduced by permission of Peter Paye **16**
Arup Associates **31, 32, 34, 35, 37, 45**
© Bruce Atherton and Jana Chiellino 2011 **42, 43, 53**
Unidentified photographers, from the Brian Boulton Collection **16, 19, 22, 23, 24**
Unidentified photographers, reproduced courtesy of the Britten–Pears Foundation (www.brittenpears.org) **21, 25, 26, 28. 29, 32, 40**
Courtesy of www.britten100.org **28, 30, 41**
James Dobing **57**
David Edwards **8, 10, 11, 12, 13, 15, 18, 27, 50, 54, 56, 57**
Evening Standard, Hulton Archive/Getty Images **39**
Maurice Foxall **42**
Sharon Goddard **44, 50, 51**
Kurt Hutton for Picture Post/Getty Images **29**
Monica Koch **49**
Nigel Luckhurst **7, 41, 46**
Rob Marrison **47**
George Rodger, Time+Life Pictures/Getty Images **27**
Reproduced by permission of Snape Parish Council **14**
The late Rosamund Strode, 1969, image reproduced courtesy of the Britten–Pears Foundation (www.brittenpears.org) **38**
Clive Strutt **32, 33, 36, 37**
Suffolk Record Office **14, 15, 16, 17, 21, 27**
Philip Vile **6, 45, 48, 51, 52, 53, 55, 56**
Malcolm Watson **41, 42, 43**
Hans Wild, 1969, Image reproduced courtesy of the Britten–Pears Foundation (www.brittenpears.org) **35**

While every attempt has been made to identify copyright holders, we regret that it has not always been possible to acknowledge all sources of material reproduced in this book.

Acknowledgments

The author would like to thank the following for their help with the researching and publication of this book: Aldeburgh Museum, Arup Associates, Jane Bellingham, Brian Boulton, Britten–Pears Foundation, Valerie Edwards, Marc Ernesti, Sharon Goddard, George Gooderham, Johnny Gooderham, Julyan Heazell, Inge Kjemtrup, Pat Lord, Graham Nicholson, Neville Patrick, Peter Paye, Louise Piffero, Ray Poacher, Jonathan Reekie, Emma Sealey, Snape Parish Council, Suffolk Record Office (Ipswich branch), Derek Sugden, Steve Tompkins, Jenni

About the author

DAVID EDWARDS was born and educated in Ipswich. After a career in theatre administration – he was chief executive of Derby Playhouse for 24 years – he returned to Suffolk in 2002 to become head of operations for what was then Aldeburgh Productions. Since retiring in 2008, he has been the chairman of the New Wolsey Theatre in Ipswich, and been involved in a number of freelance projects including DanceEast, Aldeburgh Music and the Poetry Trust. A former council member of the Theatrical Management Association, he has been a regular contributor to their house magazine, *Prompt*.